This book is dedicated to my wife and my children, whose encouragement and help allowed me to complete this tale without straying from the central message.

Seras como una luz que alumbra mi camino

- Spanish Verse

The Weavers' Legacy

Lighting the Path of Pioneers

A novel by

Stewart Baily

ISBN-13 978 1466424883
ISBN-10 1466424885

I expect to pass though this world but once. Any good therefore that I can do, or any kindness I can show to any fellow creature, let me do it now. Let me not defer or neglect it, for I shall not pass this way again.

-William Penn
Philadelphia, Pennsylvania, 1684

Chapter One

THE BROADWEAVERS

The tiny village of Bromham lies near the stark boulders of Stonehenge in the velvety pastures of Southwest England. Above the cluster of thatched cottages looms the high-pitched slate roof and steeple of the ancient church of Saint Nicholas. Its walls are blackened and weathered from nearly a thousand dreary Wiltshire winters endured since the original chapel was erected. The church lies on lands bequeathed to the Catholic Church by William the Conqueror at his death, and William's daughter Edith oversaw its construction. Over the centuries a tall spire and gothic structures were added to Saint Nicholas, but the chapel interior and small square windows betray its early Norman beginnings. It is an impressive edifice, and the only parish church for many miles in this sparsely populated countryside. The church has changed little since Daniel and Mary Baily brought their infant son, Joel, for baptism in the Anglican faith on a chilly Sunday in January 1658.

Daniel was a broadweaver living in Westbrook, a neighboring village to Bromham. The area was once a significant center for weaving because of the abundance of sheep, grazing on the gentle hills of Wiltshire. But the industry using the traditional looms was in decline, the early effects of the nascent industrial revolution. Many of Daniel's fellow weavers had already left the Wiltshire countryside for the city. The few that remained supplemented their earnings by growing fruits and vegetables for the market.

Daniel fared better than most of his neighbors. He was a yeoman, a freeholder of several parcels of land, part of an emerging middle class of England. He was able to grow food for his family and rent land to the less prosperous. The social status of Daniel and his fellow yeomen gave this group the boldness to challenge the old order of things, even the Church. However, Mary, his wife, clung more tightly to the comfort of her parent's religion. Daniel understood this. His wife was expecting their second child. Soon after Mary's delivery of a son they would call Joel, Daniel petitioned the Rector to perform the rites of baptism.

"Yeoman Daniel, it will be a pleasure," replied the Rector.

"Bring the child to Sunday's service. Your woman is well enough to make the trip?"

"Aye, Sir, she is." replied Daniel. Daniel knew that he would also need to bring a little more for the offering that day, in addition to the tithe that the Church emphatically demanded.

Mary did her best to keep her infant son warm and quiet during the service. She and Daniel sat in the rear of the sanctuary, as was the custom for their status in the community. There was no ringing of bells or smoke of incense to disturb the baby. The Anglican Church had discarded these rites decades ago.

After the service, Joel was brought forward to the baptismal font. The Rector sprinkled a few drops of water on his face and implored God to take the infant under His care. Joel did not awaken.

And so it was that Joel participated in his first religious ceremony without understanding or caring of its significance. In later years, Joel would become more questioning of religious practices. In particular, he would become infatuated with the then radical ideas of another son of a weaver, George Fox.

Who was this George Fox? Why was this ancient Catholic Church no longer providing sacraments according to the rites prescribed by Rome? And how did these events alter the way contemporary free nations view the rights of men and women? To understand all of this, we must step back from Daniel, Mary, and their infant son, Joel to the previous century. Then, curious events combined to change the way many Christians viewed their obligations to their Church and to their governments.

Saint Nicholas Parish Church, Bromham, England

Chapter Two

CHALLENGES IN MEDIEVAL EUROPE

At no time in history has Christianity been shaped so profoundly as it was in sixteenth century Europe. In 1517, in the small German City of Wittenberg, Martin Luther nailed his 95 theses to the door of a church and began a confrontation with the hierarchy of the Catholic Church that would shake it for centuries.

A monkish parish priest, Luther did not intend to create a new form of Christianity, merely establish a dialogue for change. But his actions after this challenge permitted the dialogue to expand beyond the Church hierarchy and thus beyond its control. In particular, his translation of the Bible from Latin to German permitted the educated gentry of the time to make their own moral interpretations of the biblical passages that were the teachings of Christ. The mysteries of the Gospel were no longer the privy of Latin scholars and priests. Soon, translations of the Bible, and other writings of Luther began to appear in French, English, and other languages of the continent.

The Reformation movements on the continent were very convenient to an unlikely partner of the challenge to Catholicism. King Henry VIII quarreled with the Pope, who balked at annulling Henry's marriage to the daughter of the very devout and very Catholic King of Spain. Henry responded in

1534 with the Act of Supremacy, designating the King as head of the Church in England, later to be referred to as Anglican. This bold separation from Rome provided fertile ground for the more theologically based Reformation movements, which were just beginning in England.

The remainder of the sixteenth century saw the often bloody struggles in England and in France between those seeking to restore Catholicism to its former stature, and those pressing to distance themselves from the ornate rituals and ties with Rome. New Reformation groups appeared. In England, all those who sought to purify the little-changed Anglican rites from that they deemed excessively ornate rituals were called "Puritans." The ending of this chaotic century set the stage for the next and more reflective Reformation movements. One would be called the "Religious Society of Friends" and later called derisively, "Quakers." Since "The Religious Society of Friends" was a mouthful, the Quaker label stuck. Our Quaker family would join this movement. Faith, opportunity, love, and a mixture of other forces would drive this family on a long odyssey across seas, mountains, prairies and generations to a place where they would eventually feel at peace with nature and God.

In early seventeenth century England, there were many thoughtful men who questioned the ritualistic mysticism that still surrounded the practice of Christianity, even after a century of Reformation activities. In these days it was impossible to separate religion from politics, and most Reformation activities were considered seditious. John Calvin and other prominent reformists had to conduct their activities with great caution. It was an extraordinary and dangerous time.

The plethora of theological thought was confusing to many, and especially to a young pious man named George Fox. While he was sympathetic to the views of John Calvin and his ilk, he felt that they did not go far enough. There was still too much emphasis on the rituals of worship and the interpretations of the Bible. George came from a family of modest means. George's father was a weaver, well established in his community. George's schooling was limited to the local schoolmaster's practical offerings, but George was an avid reader and eagerly consumed any literature that his family and friends could provide. He had plenty of time, too much time according to his father, to muse on philosophy and theology. He reluctantly learned his father's trade.

In 1646, George wandered the moors of Lancashire throughout the summer, trading thoughts with other Reformation activists that he encountered, and formulating his perspective on the purpose and methods of worship. George came to believe that God did not dwell in temples, but in people's hearts. He envisioned that each person could possess an "Inner Light" to guide him or her, even if one had not been exposed to Christian teaching, or had studied the Bible. While acknowledging the divine inspiration of the scriptures, the chief guide of a Christian should be the influence of the Holy Spirit in his heart.

If there was no need to attend church to communicate with God, then there was no need to offer tithes to the Church. In fact, George refused to call the edifice that worship took place in a "church." To him and his fellow Friends it was a Meeting House. The Church was a body of overcomplicated theology that he wanted no part of. These thoughts resonated with other thoughtful men and women that he encountered that summer, and he began to attract followers. He also began to attract the attention and concern of the Anglican Church.

George Fox challenged not only the theology of the time, but also the social order. Himself of modest means, he rationalized that God had made all men and women equal. There was no need to use the formal *You* or *Your Worship* when addressing the landed gentry, rather the informal *Thee* and *Thy* used heretofore only within the family or among close friends. The concept of equality among men and women was a radical concept at this time, but George passionately advocated this. His assertion that one should refuse military service or in any way harm another person was not received well among the establishment. After all, where would the King find his soldiers? Even other Puritans of the day saw his theology as blasphemy and religious anarchy.

During the period when George formulated the tenets of his theology, Oliver Cromwell, having defeated the Royalist forces in 1653, was acting as the Lord Protector of the Commonwealth of England, Scotland, and Ireland. Great leniency was granted to all branches of the Reformation movement. The Society of Friends, as George Fox called his group of followers, gathered momentum, unencumbered by government harassment.

In 1660 Charles II was restored to the throne and repressive measures began again against the Reformation, and especially against the Society of Friends, now labeled as "The Quakers." They came upon this name when one of their members replied to a magistrate that he should "Quake at the Words of the Lord!" The magistrate replied, "And you, sir, will quake at the Word of the Law!" The Friends decided this was a badge of honor, and used the term alternately with "Friends." Many Quakers faced magistrates for failing to comply with the wishes of the King and his Church. In 1662 Parliament passed "The Quaker Act" which called for imprisonment of any man or woman who professed to follow the teachings of the Society of Friends.

One prominent man of the era who was arrested for these leanings and tried in Old Bailey in London was none other than Oxford-educated William Penn, son of a high-ranking officer in the Royal Navy. He was released due to his high social standing, but it fueled his desire to find a more welcoming place where he and his Friends could practice their philosophy in peace.

To many in England at that time, the Religious Society of Friends seemed more like a philosophical group than a religion. In their austere meetings they discussed abstract concepts of right and wrong, rather than the meaning of the parables of Christ. Their drab meeting rooms rarely contained even a cross, and there was no rector or preacher. The elders of the Meeting decided when the service began, and when it was ended, shaking hands to indicate that all should go home. While they normally met on Sundays, they referred to that day as "First Day," since the English naming of the days of the week were all based on celestial objects worshiped by the pagans, or pagan gods themselves. These radical changes to the form of worship and the vernacular of the Church seemed very threatening to the Church hierarchy. The changes were very appealing to those of a more thoughtful bent.

Chapter Three

A BOY OF CURIOSITY

Joel was now nearly 13 years old, growing up happily in a large family of five brothers and sisters. One sister died in the Great Plague a few years earlier, a time of great sorrow for the family and for all of England. While most of the devastation occurred in the large cities, travelers brought the disease to the countryside, and many in Saint Nicolas' parish lost family members. The rest of the weaver's family was strong and healthy, a product of their hard work in the fields and the generous harvest from their parcels.

Joel apprenticed his father in weaving, and was a clever study. But there was only a small market for the handmade blankets and carpets that he labored over. There was increasing demand for the factory-made products with more even patterns and a greatly reduced cost. Thus, Joel found himself more and more behind his father's horses tending the several parcels near the village.

Joel loved working in the fields, and the quiet communication with nature. The renewal of the earth each spring evoked to him the promise of The Resurrection. The waves of wheat and barley rippling over the hills of Wiltshire were a sign of God's benevolence and love for the human race. He was much more comfortable here in the fields with these thoughts than in the dark pews of Saint Nicholas as the Rector rambled on with obscure allegories set in lands unfamiliar to this young Englishman.

Daniel would read the Bible each night to his large family. The King James Version of the Bible had been published earlier in the seventeenth century and the Baily family was among the few in town who could afford one. Joel enjoyed listening to the stories, but he had many questions.

"Father, how could Christ make loaves of bread multiply? Everyone knows that wheat is needed to make bread, and this requires a season of tending. Wine from water? The grapes must be crushed!"

Joel's interruptions annoyed Daniel.

"Thee must have faith, my son." replied Daniel. "Not everything in the scriptures is intended for thee to understand. The Rector will explain their meaning."

Joel was not satisfied. The meaning should not be obscured so that only a few privileged and highly educated people could make sense of the scriptures. There must to be an easier path to enlightenment, he thought. Joel firmly believed in God. How else could the wonders of nature come to be, if not from the hand of a powerful spiritual being? But what did God want from his creations?

Joel continued to attend Saint Nicolas because he knew it pleased his mother. He met other young men and women of his own age, and developed his social skills, He learned of the scandalous activities of George Fox and the other reformists.

Sitting among the tombstones that encircled Saint Nicholas, he and his friends traded stories of the progress of the Reformation in other parts of England, whispering so that the Rector would not interfere.

Joel learned that George Fox was conducting a Meeting that weekend in the ancient city of Bath, only ten miles from Westbrook. He decided to find out what this "Inner Light" was all about. Over the next few days, Joel was mesmerized by Fox's very direct and powerful logic. Everything one needed to please God and mankind was already within every person. All that was necessary was to learn to listen to your own heart! Joel joined the growing group of Friends in Wiltshire.

Chapter Four

THE EMMIGRATION

When Charles II was restored to the crown, an uneasy peace ensued. While Charles II was technically a Protestant, he wanted the Church of England to restore many of the discarded sacraments and services. Prosecution of the Puritans began anew. It was during this period that many of the Reformation groups began the thought that if they wanted to worship the way they felt was right, they would have to leave England. After all, the settlement in Plymouth had gone well, after a rough start. A few Quaker families had joined that settlement, but were not treated well by the original Pilgrims. The King was eager to enrich his coffers with the products from the colonies, having exhausted the treasury with wars within and without his kingdom. In fact, he was also eager to settle his debts with large grants of land in the colonies that many felt were of little value.

The King owed a great deal of money to the estate of Admiral Penn, whose son was now a leader in the movement of the Society of Friends. A large parcel of land in the middle Atlantic area was granted to William Penn II for the purpose of a secular settlement. The Quakers had found a home at last!

In 1682 William Penn and a group of 100 Quaker settlers arrived in the Delaware River off the shore of what is now the city of Chester. These settlers were men and women of means and were able to purchase their passage and the supplies needed to begin a settlement in a new land. Joel Baily was not among this group.

Back in Westbrook there were other things on Joel's mind. Joel's father had died while Joel was only 16. His older brother Daniel, had assumed the weaving business, but the market was not large enough to support his new growing family, and his remaining brothers and sisters. It was time for Joel to make a life of his own. He awoke one morning, sure that the Inner Light had shown him a way. He shared his thoughts with Daniel.

"Brother, I must leave thee and go where there are others who feel as I do about the worship of God." he said. "It saddens me to leave Wiltshire, but I am told that the new land that Penn calls "Penn's Woods" is also very beautiful and fertile."

"Aye brother, I understand. There is very little future for thee in this village. I will help thee as much as I can." Daniel would keep his word, too.

Joel learned that William Penn had provided for a system of indentured service whereby land would be received for those who completed a relatively short service. It would be called the "Holy Experiment". Joel saw the solution to his material and spiritual quandaries. He found in 1683, a lad of his own age from Bromham named Thomas Withers. Thomas's father had purchased 500 acres from Penn's agents in Delaware County only 40 miles from the new port of Philadelphia that was sprouting along the Delaware River. That amount of land would require a great deal of labor to develop, and Thomas welcomed the help of this strong young yeoman in this endeavor. In the spring of 1684, the two made the trek to the small port of Deal, Kent, laden with tools, seed, and high hopes of success in the New World.

The port of Deal was located on the English Channel, a week's journey by foot for the two young men. As they arrived, they made out the ominous outline of Deal Castle brooding over the port, cannon facing in all directions. Built by King Henry VIII in the previous century, it was one of the key fortifications along the coast. Fishing boats bobbed in the harbor and moved about the small channel to the sea. The area around the wharf was filled with stalls selling the bounty of the sea and fresh produce from the neighboring farmland. This was a daunting sight for the two lads used to the pastoral tranquility of Wiltshire.

They spotted their passage to America, the brig *Antelope* taking on supplies for the voyage. At that moment, the reality of their adventure became evident.

While it dwarfed the fishing vessels that passed its mooring, the *Antelope* seemed small for an ocean voyage to Joel. The prow of the ship was only several yards above the waterline and the deck had barely enough room for the winches and tackle being tugged earnestly by a rather scruffy crew. However, he remembered this was the sister ship to the *Welcome* that safely carried William Penn on his first voyage. Since that time more that 2000 English and Irish Quaker emigrants had been ferried to the new colony. Thomas and Joel shouldered their bags and headed for the gangway at amidships. They were shown to their bunks forward of the cargo deck in an open area where they had to stoop to move about. Families were the only ones with the luxury of privacy in the sleeping quarters. This usually was offered only by a heavy drape. Upon departure, there were nearly one hundred men, women, and children of the Quaker movement aboard.

English Sailing Ship of the *Antelope* Class

Chapter 5

THE VOYAGE

The North Atlantic is typically choppy, and this was the experience for the first few days of Joel's voyage. The small vessel plunged through the seas, sending a misty salty spray over all those who tried to stay on the main deck. Below was little better as the passengers coped with acute seasickness in the cramped and foul-smelling cargo deck. Gradually, Joel gained his sea legs and spent most of the time watching the British Isles disappear below the horizon.

The young unmarried men amused themselves playing cards and telling stories. The diversity of the voyagers amazed Joel. Farmers, merchants, educated professionals were leaving all that they knew to make a life in the New World. Joel admitted to himself that he was not a little apprehensive. He had heard of savages terrorizing the settlers. And what if one's crops should fail? Family and friends were a long ocean journey away!

Joel was unsure why he felt that he was on the right path, but his heart was content. He knew that the light from the western sunset was beckoning to him. It seemed far away, but it was as strong as the Inner Light that now burned within him.

The ship's master did his best to avoid violent storms, and was fairly successful. However, this added additional time for the crossing. Meals became more difficult to endure. The grain for biscuits became wormy. The cider became vinegar. Joel and Tim reminisced about their mothers' cooking. When would this voyage end? It was nearly two months before the ship entered the Delaware River and began the northward course to the new port of Philadelphia. The excitement of the passengers grew, as green forests and low rolling hills replaced the monotonous scenery of the sea. On June 10, 1783, the *Antelope* dropped anchor off the shore of the new capital city of Pennsylvania.

Joel and Thomas were excited to see that activity at the water's edge. The city had been laid out with wide boulevards in precise squares according to Penn's instructions.   Its principal commercial area was Market Street that stretched from the waterfront to the Schuykill River. Buildings along the wharf stood three stories high, and were alive with men hoisting kegs and boxes of cargo on long booms fitted with pulleys. Here they could find all of the supplies they would need to begin clearing land for crops.

They hurried down the gangway with their belongings tied on their backs, eager for the feel of solid ground. They spotted a fish market at the end of the wharf overflowing with fresh fish from the river - bass, bluefish, mussels, crabs and other creatures they did not recognize. There were fishmongers standing behind steaming pots ready too cook your order, and the two young men did not hesitate. Joel and Thomas ate their first meal in the New World sitting on a crude bench by the roadside. The next day they would begin to negotiate for horses and other supplies for their final leg of the journey.

The Weavers' Legacy

Chapter Six

CHESTER COUNTY, PENNSYLVANIA, 1686

Joel prodded his horse gently down the bank to a rippling stream and stopped to let the animal drink. It was a hot spring day, and they had traveled far. He patted his saddlebag to assure himself that the precious document was still there, a deed to 150 acres of land in the gently rolling hills of Chester County, Pennsylvania. He had purchased the land through his efforts of working the farm of Thomas Withers, and with a small loan from his brother Daniel back in Wiltshire.

His gaze followed the stream known as Oldman's Creek that meandered its way down a shallow valley flanked with poplar and oak trees. *A perfect place to graze livestock,* he thought, *and plenty of wood for fences and outbuildings!* He could not help but to think of Wiltshire, how remarkably similar the landscapes were. *But this is thy home now!* He dug his heels into the mare's withers and galloped to the campsite he had established a week before

Joel spent the summer and fall clearing land and constructing shelter for himself and his small stock of cows, pigs and chickens. Game was plentiful, and he became an excellent marksman. The excess of his hunting and gardening was readily sold in the nearby village of Marlboro. With his earnings he was able to hire the craftsmen to finish off his structures with a professional flourish. By first snow, he was snug in a very handsome farmstead. Then he turned himself to the task of becoming a respected member of the community.

During the nastier days of winter, he busied himself with a handmade loom, making rugs and window coverings. He had not forgotten the skills his father and brother had taught him. He sometimes took in weaving work from neighbors who admired his colorful patterns. His neighbors playfully called him "The Weaver," even though he spent far more time doing farm chores.

The nearest Friends Meetinghouse was in Chichester, nine miles away. He made the trek faithfully every month throughout the dreary winter and was an active participant in the Meetings, and the community projects that the group undertook. The Meetinghouse was built in the style of the day. There was one row of pews along the back of the room for the elders. Facing these were ten rows of pews for the remaining members of the Meeting. One wood stove provided barely adequate heat in the winter. In the summer, all the windows were open, and a chorus of songbirds provided cheery relief to the silence that characterized the Meeting.

During his third visit he met a young unmarried woman named Ann Short. Ann had arrived in Pennsylvania along with her parents and a sister with the first voyage of William Penn on the *Welcome*. She was witty and outspoken, and she was lovely, even with her sandy hair severely tied back in the fashion of Quakers ladies, tucked under a white bonnet. Joel was smitten, and committed himself even more to the activities of the Meeting. It became apparent that Ann had reciprocal feelings for the fair-haired, blue-eyed young farmer. In the late spring the two announced their intentions to be married before the Meeting, as required by custom.

Joel had chosen well. His new wife was as industrious as she was charming, and the farm prospered. The work to improve the land was arduous: moving boulders, clearing brush, felling trees. Joel was grateful for the experience he had with Tom Withers clearing the land. Each year the pastures grew larger, and the tillable soil became plentiful. Corn, barley, and alfalfa waved from every corner of the farm. Over the years Joel acquired adjoining lands, and by 1720, their holdings totaled over 600 acres. Their family had increased as well. They now had eight children - six sturdy boys and two comely girls to perform the seemingly endless chores that accrue on such a large spread. The lad from Wiltshire was now a successful farmer and an elder, a respected member of the Religious Society of Friends in the Province of Pennsylvania.

Joel died in 1724, leaving his sizable estate to his male heirs. The girls had married well. Joel made sure that Ann was well provided for. Each of his sons used their inheritance wisely, starting new farms, and entering related agriculturally based businesses. Their third-born son, Joel's namesake, married the same year of his father's death and moved his new wife, Betty, onto part of the family homestead. This will be this branch of the family that the Inner Light would move the strongest and the longest.

Settler's Cabin in Frontier America

Chapter Seven

FORMATIVE YEARS IN PENNSYLVANIA

The English crown was content to leave the peace-loving Province of Pennsylvania, as it was then called, to govern itself. The produce of the land, timbers for shipbuilding, and sales of English goods enriched the coffers of the King, who was wise enough not to tamper with success. There were few problems with the Delaware and Lenape Indians, as they had been treated honorably by William Penn in land dealings. Penn insisted that all others in the provincial government follow his example.

The farm families of the Quakers, the Amish, and the Mennonites were large, and the land under cultivation rapidly increased into the surrounding counties, namely, Bucks, Lancaster, and York. Collectively, the English-decent Quakers, and German-decent Amish and Mennonites were known in the Colonies as the "Plain Sects." They eschewed the bright plaids and patterns of the day's fashions for the somber black and gray, especially in the countryside. In the cities, Quakers were worldlier in dress and in speech, and were generally from more prosperous backgrounds.

The broad Susquehanna River, which ran from the New York border to the Chesapeake Bay, provided economical transportation for bringing the products to neighboring colonies and for export. The land beyond the Susquehanna formed in waves of low mountains called the Appalachian Range. This land was suited for grazing animals, and trappers, but not the grain crops demanded by the growing population.

It turned out that Quakers were excellent merchants and craftsman, as well as farmers. Philadelphia became a prosperous mercantile center, with fleets of ships to carry the produce of Pennsylvania to shores other than just England. Some of the good will among settlers in the early years gave way, as the good lands in the eastern part of the colony became crowded with new arrivals. Border disputes with Maryland became more frequent. Succeeding generations began to look west for opportunity, and the quieter life their families once had.

In 1776 the American Revolution officially arrived in Pennsylvania. Joel's grandchildren of fighting age clung to their pacifist beliefs and did not take up arms, even though there was a great deal of pressure from neighbors of other Christian denominations. Isaac Baily was, even so, a strong supporter of the fight for independence. Isaac's father, Joel's namesake son, had shared with Isaac the "Common Sense" pamphlets of Thomas Paine, which made good sense to them as well. Isaac's father died in 1775 as the rebellion in Massachusetts reached a boil.

In July of 1776 Isaac read the words of the Declaration of Independence, displayed on the front of the courthouse in West Chester. He mouthed the words *"... that all men are created equal"* and thought: *These words were written also by George Fox over a century ago!* Isaac resolved to help the Revolution in ways that he could without the use of arms. He provided Washington's quartermasters with supplies, and with his wife Lydia, provided water, fruit and other comfort to the weary Colonial soldiers passing to and from the frequent skirmishes that occurred very close to their homestead.

The British had deployed the fierce Hessian soldiers in a ring around Philadelphia to protect the troops that were quartered there. General Washington tried several times to break that ring, and one of the fiercest battles took place along the small Brandywine River near Isaac's farm. During the Battle of the Brandywine in 1777, Lydia and Isaac could hear the cannon and were frightened for their lives. Some of their neighbors were attending the Meetinghouse near the Brandywine River when the battle commenced. Shells hit the stone structure from both sides, but the Friends were unharmed. The battle did not go well for the Colonials. Washington wisely retreated. A decisive victory for the British at that point could have put an end to the Revolution.

The passage of soldiers and other men supporting the Revolution had a strong effect on Isaac's young son Vincent. The soldiers told of the lands that stretched beyond the Appalachian Mountains, all the way to a great river called the Mississippi. The soil was rich, and most untouched by a plow or scythe. The few white men that inhabited this land were hunters and trappers. Large land holdings could be purchased for the same price that a small farmstead would bring in Eastern Pennsylvania. These tales evoked images that the young Vincent would carry with him as he sat in the Meetinghouse on First Days. The Quaker meetings of a farm community usually provoked little interesting discussion or philosophy, as they were far from the active political churnings of Philadelphia. Thus, Vincent would fill the time of the mostly silent meetings in reflection, daydreaming of moving westward to a land with endless horizons. He did not consider this disrespectful to God. His father had often told him it was the Inner Spirit that put ideas in the minds of men. His dreaming would not be fulfilled for many years.

When Vincent became an adult, he farmed for many years on a parcel of his father's farm. He married a woman from the nearby Meeting, Susanna Bernard, an adventuresome woman five years his junior. Susanna encouraged Vincent to try new things, as it was apparent that her husband was not happy to stay on his father's lands. They moved to a location along the Maryland border near the narrow neck of the Chesapeake Bay and established a successful General Store. They started a family that eventually grew to three sons and two daughters.

The land where the store was located was in an area that was long contested between the State of Maryland and the State of Pennsylvania prior to the Revolutionary War. The surveyors Mason and Dixon had determined a boundary at the behest of the Crown, but still many Quakers had settled there, thinking that they were in their home state. Catholic immigrants from Lord Baltimore's Maryland settlements also started homesteads. Some of the more wealthy settlers also had slaves.

Although the families of all faiths tried to be good neighbors, the differences in the two groups became an obstacle. The plain garb of the Quakers contrasted with the more contemporary dress of the Catholic families. The concept of slavery was also repugnant to the Quakers, who believed that all men and women were created equal. In the markets and other public places where the Catholics and Quakers co-mingled, discussions of these topics were inevitable and unpleasant. Gradually, some Quaker families, including Vincent and Susanna, began to realize that this was not an environment that they wanted for their families. Vincent thought back to the dreams of his youth, and began looking for land opportunities. In time he found a place that met his expectations. The Light beckoned west, just as it had for his grandfather, Joel.

Chapter Eight

TAZEWELL COUNTY ILLINOIS

In 1829, Vincent, now in his early 50's, arrived in Tazewell County, Illinois, near the small town of Delevan, with the intention of returning to farming. Vincent's long beard was flecked with gray, but his body was lean and strong. He had secured 80 acres of land in the high prairie west of the town. Vincent and Susanna brought with them their youngest son, Jeremiah, the only member of their family who had not by then married. Vincent would need his son's help in the establishing of a new homestead. Jeremiah was eager to begin a new adventure.

Railroads were just getting established in the eastern seaboard, and none extended beyond the Appalachian Mountains at that time. Most of their journey had been by "Prairie Schooner," a sturdy wagon made in Pennsylvania's Conestoga Valley by Mennonite craftsmen. It carried prodigious amounts of furniture, tools, and kitchen gear. Vincent was able to sell it easily, to families who were headed even further West.

They had chosen Tazewell County because there was already a small community of Friends in this area, and they knew that if they needed help or advice, it would be offered freely. They chose to stock their farm primarily with beef cattle and hogs, as these animals required much less care then the dairy cows that his father had tended. Susanna was in charge of the chickens and the large vegetable plot that surrounded the sod home and outbuildings they had crafted. As they approached their first fall in Illinois, they were very pleased with the bounty of their harvest, and the prices that were obtained for their livestock.

The homesteads of the early settlers of Illinois were typically distant from one another, and the same applied to the small group of Friends that settled in Tazewell County. It was impractical to arrange a Meeting every week because of the long distances for travel. Instead there was a Monthy Meeting held in the larger town of Pekin, about a half-day's travel for most of the settlers who adopted an agricultural life. This event was eagerly anticipated by all. Not only was there an opportunity to socialize, but there was the need to buy supplies, take produce to market, and learn of news from other parts of the world. Normally, the families would make camp near the town for the weekend.

The big news for the settlers in Illinois and other parts of the frontier lands was the activity of the Indian tribes in the area. Congress had just passed in 1830, the "Indian Treaty and Removal Act" The net effect of this act was to legitimize U.S. troops and militia to push the native Indians further west, past the Mississippi River. While Susanna and Vincent had themselves few problems with Indians, they had heard of other families that had been terrorized and robbed by bands of Chippewa Indians who felt that the white men were trespassing on their hunting grounds. When word of the new treaty reached the Indian population in Tazewell County, most of the Chippewas decided to follow their leaders westward. A few refused, and some skirmishes occurred between the renegades and the settlers.

The arrival of troops of cavalry in the summer of 1830 in Pekin removed most of the danger. All of the Quaker men had rifles for hunting and to ward off varmints around their farms, but firmly believed in peaceful cooperation with the native Indians, just as William Penn had taught in Pennsylvania in the early settlements. They were saddened to see the Indian families forced westward.

Winter approaches quickly on the prairie. The Bailys had prepared a large root cellar for their winter stores. Dried fruit, squash, beans, potatoes, and other produce from their land was laid in abundance for the long winter season. Vincent, Susanna, and Jeremiah were proud of how quickly they had adapted to frontier life. They would be tested on these skills.

The winter of 1830-1831 in Tazewell County was the fiercest that any of the settlers could remember. They called it the "Winter of the Deep Snow." The snow fell heavily in late November and continued intermittently for weeks. Then, the winds from the western prairie began howling and piled the snow in rows resembling breakers rolling in from the ocean, 30 feet high in some places. The snow piled up around the outbuildings and dwellings of the settlers. Often only a smoking chimney remained to indicate that there was life on the prairie.

Vincent and Jeremiah dug out paths from their home to the outbuildings to allow them to tend to the livestock. The road to Delavan, however, seven miles distant, was hopelessly drifted in. They would have to make do with the items in their carefully prepared root cellar until the road was clear. It was to be six weeks before an early thaw permitted travel to Delevan to replenish their supplies. Susanna performed miracles making appetizing meals from dried and canned vegetables and fruit, but what they all missed was bread. The only mill was in Delevan, and while the Bailys had plenty of grain stored for the winter, the only way it could be consumed was in soups or stews.

In the spring, the Bailys were finally able to attend the Monthly Meeting in Pekin. There was great joy among the Friends to see that their small community had survived the winter, and for a change, many of the attendees during the long

33

hour of fellowship had something to say. Jeremiah was grateful that he did not have to endure the long periods of silence that normally occurred during Meeting. He also found most interesting a young woman who was moved by the Inner Light to speak. She was very articulate. Her name was Miriam Brown, and her Quaker roots were from an emigration even earlier than the Baily's arrival. Jeremiah admired also her sparkling eyes and shy smile.

Jeremiah and Miriam had a long courtship, owing to the distances between their families. They declared their intention to marry the following spring at the Monthly Meeting. With the help of his father, Jeremiah acquired acreage adjoining the homestead. Father and son were excellent farmers, and the farm prospered. Jeremiah's marriage also prospered. Jeremiah and Mary produced three sons and two daughters. Their family life and spiritual life was fulfilling. But the clouds of Civil War were on the horizon. While no one in Delevan kept slaves, passions were high. Jeremiah and Miriam became an integral part of the" Underground Railroad" intent on keeping their sons from the fighting in the east, although many Illinois boys were recruited.

The Underground Railroad was very active in Illinois before and during the Civil War. Runaway slaves from the South generally followed the rivers north. Members of the Underground Railroad movement would search for them along the riverbanks and bring them to safe houses such as the Baily's farm for safekeeping during the day. The runaways would be hidden in one of the outbuildings, and provided with food and water. It was dangerous, because the slave-owners had offered rewards for the runaways, and the men seeking those rewards were men of low moral character. Jeremiah and Miriam persisted in the enterprise, because they knew it was right. Most of the slaves were heading to Chicago, where there was ample work for unskilled labor

Jeremiah and Miriam's oldest son Joseph was eager to make a

more direct contribution and join the Union Army. However, he bowed to his parents' wishes. He was restless, though, and found himself wanting to explore beyond Illinois. If not East, then why not West? But he focused first his attention on farming.

Joseph took over the farm upon his father's death. He married Priscilla Haines, a woman he had met at the Monthly Meeting in Pekin. She had been raised in Illinois on the high prairie, and was acclimated to the wilderness and the hard life of a frontier settler. They toiled on the farm for 15 years, increasing its acreage to 240 acres.

Joseph and Priscilla longed for closer contact with their relatives in the east, and often wrote to encourage them to join them on the prairie. In 1874, Joseph wrote to his cousin:

I have been almost 20 years from your state. I think thee would do well to come here. Our land is unquestionably rich and fertile as your land. The large streams are like the Susquehanna. There are but few Friends in this state and just two Meetings. One is about 50 miles to the north, and the other about the same to the south. I would like to see more settling here...

But he did not succeed in attracting any more relatives or Friends. Finally, he and Priscilla decided that the land to the West beckoned. It did not take long to find another location.

Chapter Nine

WACO MISSOURI, 1883-1893

Joseph Baily dismounted from his buckboard and scanned the horizon, fascinated by the green knolls and flowering meadows of Western Missouri. He was amazed that land could be acquired so cheaply. He had sold his farm in Delevan and with the proceeds had purchased 640 acres of Missouri land very suitable for grazing. He was now 45 years old. He brought with him his wife, Priscilla, and their family of two sons and two daughters. The boys were already strong enough to handle a team of horses, and other heavy farm chores. The girls pitched in to help their mother, and with other lighter tasks around the farm.

Life west of the Mississippi was similar to that in Illinois, except that neighbors were even further away, and opportunities for socializing were few. Friends meetings were held in the town of Joplin, about an hour's drive in the buckboard for the family. One of Joseph and Priscilla's daughters, Mercy, met a young man, a Friend from Pennsylvania who was visiting family in Joplin. They soon married and she was happy to return with him to Pennsylvania where life was not so rustic. The older son,

Clarence, decided that farming was not for him. He joined a mining company and pursued the oil-rich shale formations that were so abundant in this region and the neighboring territories. The younger son, Edwin, and his sister, Fannie, were content to help their parents run the large spread over the next few years.

Edwin was a well-built young man, tall in stature, with a strong jaw and penetrating steel-blue eyes that caused many a flutter among the young girls in Meeting. They would approach Fannie at the socials to find out if Edwin had a secret sweetheart, and she would just smile. Edwin was a serious youth and found more interest in the cultivation of fruit trees and ways to increase the yield of crops. This would all change later

In the 1890's, terrible times came to the frontier settlements. Hordes of grasshoppers decimated their crops. This was followed by several years of severe drought. Farmers were forced to greatly reduce their size of their herds and the amount of land under cultivation. They had to borrow for seed for the next seasons, and banks were skittish to lend, having just endured one of the longest and most severe depressions the young United States had ever endured. Joseph and Priscilla mortgaged their property and tried to hang on. After a few years, it became clear that they could not keep the farm as a going concern.

They prayed nightly for some insight from the Inner Light. Finally, they received a letter from their older son, Clarence, describing a place in Kansas that he had discovered while searching for oil with his mining company. This was the sign they were looking for. They sold the farm at an unfavorable price, paid off the remaining mortgage, and resolved to begin again in a place more conducive to a simple life of growing crops.

Chapter Ten

SPRING HILL, KANSAS, 1895 - 1898

Spring Hill was a small farming community, one day's ride south of Kansas City. It was blessed with an ample water supply, and a railroad stop was located not far from town. With the proceeds from the farm in Missouri, Joseph was able to purchase a 160-acre dairy farm from the widow of the previous owner. It was of a size that he and Priscilla could easily manage on his own. Edwin sought and found work on a neighboring ranch. Fannie found work as a clerk in the town's only general store.

In Kansas, the Quaker men had abandoned the plain dark garb that characterized the Quakers in the East, and dressed in the more comfortable overalls and loose-fitting shirts that the other settlers wore. The summers were hot and dusty, and the work was strenuous. Fannie and her mother also adopted the dress styles of the frontier. When the infrequent Friends Meetings were organized, the family dressed more formally in the old style.

The town was typical of communities on the Great Plains. There were liveries, several blacksmiths, a hardware store, and the usual assortment of saloons, haberdashery shops, and boarding houses. There were only a few hundred dwellings. The clientele was drawn from the farms and ranches that stretched into the horizon. The land was mostly flat, but there were knolls to the west that protected the town from the winds that howled steadily during winter months. Stands of cottonwood and sycamores lined the small river at the edge of town. The nearest city was Olathe on the old Santa Fe Trail, just 20 miles west. Olathe boasted a population exceeding 3500 people.

Kansas was a rough and ready territory compared with its neighboring states to the east. Renegade Indian bands still terrorized settlers in parts of the countryside. Rustlers, bandits and other troublemakers roamed the lands. Even peace-loving Quakers found it necessary to carry firearms and travel in groups beyond the settlements.

Edwin rode the range, herding cattle. He slept on the open range at night, watching for rustlers and wolves. It was a lonely existence. He had lots of time to think. Edwin was not particularly happy to be a hired hand, even though his employer, a devout Methodist, treated him very well. He understood that he would eventually inherit his father's farm, but that seemed distant, and, frankly, not inspiring. Life in Southeastern Kansas proceeded agonizingly slowly for the young unmarried man of 25. *Surely there was something more!*

Joseph and Priscilla in their later years in Kansas

Chapter Eleven

WAR NEWS!

In February 1898, Edwin bought a newspaper that arrived with the stagecoach from Olathe. The Battleship Maine had been blown up in Havana harbor! 266 members of the crew were killed. Tensions between the USA and Spain had been strained for some time, but this event galvanized the nation. Congress was calling for retaliation. Edwin knew his parents and friends in the small Friends Meeting in Spring Hill would be calling for reconciliation, but he was infuriated by the insult to the United States.

In May 1898 there was a formal announcement calling for volunteers to join the 22nd Kansas Infantry Regiment in Norton, with immediate shipment to an East Coast training camp. Edwin did not hesitate. He told his parents that evening of his decision. Priscilla reminded him that if he put on a uniform he would be disowned by the Meeting.

"Mama, I know this, but my heart tells me that my country's needs must come first!" exclaimed Edwin. Joseph just nodded his head. When he was younger he had the same feelings in the fight against slavery, but had acquiesced to his parent's wishes.

The family prayed before dinner that night, but nothing was said of Edwin's departure.

Several days later, Joseph drove Edwin in the buckboard to the train that would set him on his way to induction in the infantry. It would be Edwin's first train ride.

As they stood on the platform awaiting the train, they said very little. Joseph had always been a taciturn man, but he seemed quieter than usual. Finally the train chugged into the station in a swirl of steam. Edwin turned to his father: "Farewell, Papa. Thank thee for understanding. I promise to comport myself well."

"Fare thee well my son." said Joseph. "Be careful, and be sure to write thy Mother often. She will worry about thee." With that, the father and son shook hands, and Edwin leapt into the car. Joseph waited until the train disappeared around the knolls. Then he turned the rig back toward Spring Hill.

Edwin arrived in Norton with only the clothes he wore and a small traveling bag of sundries. He and the other recruits expected to be issued uniforms right away, but these had not yet arrived. After a brief mustering in ceremony the 22nd Kansas Volunteer Infantry drilled in civilian clothes, using sticks for firearms. The following week, May 7, 1898, wearing fresh uniforms, the group was loaded on a train with the final destination Camp Alger, located on the Virginia side of Washington DC, for advanced training in preparation of the assault on Cuba. Edwin looked very impressive in his new infantry uniform, little changed from the Union Civil war issue. He wished his parents and sister could see him now!

Chapter Twelve

EASTERN BOUND

The trip east took four days, with many changes of locomotives. Edwin watched the terrain change from flat plains to rolling prairie, to the lush pastures and tidy towns of Ohio and Pennsylvania. He wondered what drove his grandparents to leave these lands for the sparsely populated frontier. He wondered if life for his Quaker forefathers had been as difficult in Pennsylvania, as it was for his family now in Kansas.

While passing through the Cumberland Pass in the Appalachian Mountains, they learned that their destination had been changed. Typhoid had broken out in Camp Alger. The new recruits were to be sent to Camp Meade, across the Susquehanna River from Harrisburg, Pennsylvania. Edwin was delighted. His sister, Mercy, had settled with her husband near Harrisburg. The only contact with Mercy since Waco, Missouri had been through correspondence, and the letters were weeks old by the time they reached the family. Perhaps there would be time for leave, and a personal visit. It would please his mother.

The officers made it clear, however, that leave was out of the question. The U.S. Marines had landed in Guantanamo Bay. The U.S. Army was expected to lead the assault on Havana. The Kansas Volunteers had only just received their weapons, Springfield 30-caliber bolt-action rifles, which were somewhat dated, but seemed marvelously deadly to the young Kansans. The officers realized that there was little time to prepare them for a battle with seasoned Spanish troops.

The days passed quickly, with early reveilles and mock skirmishes along the banks of the Susquehanna until the early evening. It was hot and humid and each night the soldiers bathed gratefully in the big river. Edwin wrote detailed descriptions of life in an Army camp to his family, by lantern light in his tent:

Dear Mama and Papa. Just received your letter. You ask me what I like best, Army life or farming. I like farming best. I did not come for a snap or to get out of work but to help Uncle Sam whip the Spaniard. And I am one of the boys who can do it if he gives me a chance. But I don't think he will give me a chance. We are wasting our time here running through the woods at breakneck speeds yelling like Indians. We had a gun inspection today and the Major said that there was not a gun fit for inspection. Your son, Ed

In July they learned that Teddy Roosevelt and his Rough Riders had made the charge up San Juan Hill, capturing the primary defenses for the Cuban City of Santiago. Other Army units had invaded Puerto Rico with little resistance. The Philippines had been effectively captured by the U.S. Navy's blockade of Manila's harbor. Slowly it dawned on the Volunteers of the 22nd Infantry Regiment, Kansas, that the war would probably be over by the time their training had ended. In early September they learned that the U.S. Flag had been raised over Havana. The Volunteers of the 22nd Kansas Infantry Regiment would be mustered out within the month.

Edwin (center with cigar) and his Kansas Volunteer Infantry Platoon

Chapter Thirteen

A FAMILY VISIT

Edwin was finally able to secure a week's pass to visit his sister Mercy. She and her husband, Frederick Cauffman, lived on the opposite shore of the Susquehanna, very near the Maryland border in a town called Wakefield, in Lancaster County. Edwin took a ferry across the river at the crossing and set off on foot south toward Maryland. Wearing his infantry uniform, he received rides from friendly farmers and merchants and reached Wakefield by noon the next day. Mercy was overjoyed to see her younger brother. She was concerned, though, what members of the Meeting would say when they spotted the uniform. Her husband, a respected furniture maker and undertaker in the town, provided Edwin with less conspicuous clothing.

Edwin and his sister's family spent the week visiting with neighbors and distant relatives that Edwin had learned about from his parents or grandparents. Now these relatives had faces. Everyone was very welcoming. Upon learning that Edwin was not happy with his life in Kansas, they encouraged him to seek work in Lancaster County.

Edwin went to Meeting with the Cauffmans on Sunday to a place called Penn Hill, near Wakefield. He learned that the red brick Meetinghouse had been built by one of his close relatives.

It was a plain but attractive building set on a small knoll, with a wide porch surrounding on three sides, similar to many that were built in that period. Edwin sat on the hard wooden pew and listened as the Lancaster County Friends individually spoke their hearts about the blessings of their families, their crops, or whatever the Inner Light moved them to say. Edwin was moved as well. He stood and said that he felt God had led him here to this beautiful place, with such welcoming people. He felt at home. He announced that he had decided to find work here and would like to be welcomed into this Meeting. After this sudden announcement, no one else was moved to speak, and the Elders shook hands, ending the Meeting.

As the Friends gathered on the porch to socialize, a tall elderly man walked up to Edwin and introduced himself. "I am Joshua, Edwin." he said. "My neighbor has a large dairy farm and I know he is seeking a strong lad like yourself to help manage his estate. I can introduce thee. His name is John Scott, and he is Presbyterian, and an honest man."

Edwin quickly agreed to meet this potential employer. He said his farewells to his sister and her family, and climbed up on the seat next to Joshua. The buggy moved out smartly along the dusty road toward a part of Lancaster County called "Little Britain."

John Scott's estate was called "Scott's Manor", and it was far more than just a dairy farm. There were orchards, a gristmill, a black smith shop, and many outbuildings for other crafts. John had inherited this estate from his father, a Revolutionary War officer under Washington who received a promotion for heroism in the battles at Brandywine and Germantown. The family was very respected, and very wealthy, thanks to the shrewd financial skills that so often, it seems, bless the Scots.

The introduction went well. The fact that Edwin had eagerly put on a uniform to fight for his country despite his Quaker heritage impressed John, whose family was fiercely patriotic.

Harvest time was imminent: How soon could Edwin begin work? Edwin said, "I must return to Harrisburg to obtain my release. I can return within the week." In this sudden fashion, the boy who was raised on the prairie started a new life as an eastern farmer, very near the place where his ancestors had tilled the land over two centuries ago.

It took several days to complete the paperwork of mustering out of the Kansas Volunteers. The officers grumbled, but their mission was over, and it seemed senseless to return the soldier to Kansas if he had decided to stay here. A harder job was to write his parents and his sister of his decision.

Dear Folks. I have secured a position as foreman for a very large landowner near Mercy's home in Lancaster County. Mr. Scott uses all the latest techniques for farming and I can learn much in his employ. The family is very kind. They have provided me with comfortable quarters on their estate. I miss thee very much but I feel that the Inner Light has led me to this place. Give my best to all that enquire. I will write again soon...Ed

Chapter Fourteen

SCOTT'S MANOR

Several years passed by. Edwin barely noticed. He was up before sunrise every morning with the cows, and spent the afternoons driving a team of mules to plant or harvest crops. Evenings were spent repairing equipment by lantern light, until he drifted off to sleep.

The Scott family often invited him to share the Sunday repast with them. Edwin was pleased to accept, because it gave him the opportunity to see Mary, their daughter. Mary was promised to another man, a Frank Aulthouse, from a nearby town. Edwin was nevertheless happy to have her at the table. Mary had tutors who had schooled her in literature, the sciences, and geography. Edwin's own schooling had been limited to the three 'R's. It was fascinating to hear Mary explain patiently how the rest of the world lived and worked.

When Mary left to marry her fiancée, Edwin threw himself back into his work. Yes, there were young women he would meet at socials or in stores, but none held his interest for very long. He spent more time with his sister's family in Wakefield. After the harvest season, he made the trek back to Kansas to see Fannie and his parents. It was pleasant to visit, but he found that his heart was still back in Pennsylvania.

The following year, there was shocking news at Scott's Manor. Mary's husband had suddenly died! No one knew exactly how this happened. He awoke one morning complaining of pain in his intestines, and was dead by nightfall. The doctor wrote "internal infection" on the death certificate. A funeral service was held in the Little Britain Presbyterian Church. Mary returned to Scott's Manor in black mourning clothing.

Edwin knew he must respect the mourning period. He was circumspect while attending the Sunday dinners while Mary was there. But slowly, the old Mary began to emerge, discussing literature and the latest science discoveries that appeared in the newspapers.

Gradually, Mary began to spend more time discussing these things with Edwin alone.

Mary Hanna Scott

Chapter 15

CHESTER COUNTY, PENNSYLVANIA, 1906

Mary and Edwin drove the little black buggy along the dusty roads that led from Scott's Manor in Lancaster County to East Nottingham Township in Chester County. It was a sporty vehicle, and the sleek chestnut mare moved the couple over the rolling hills that pervade this landscape in less that two hours. They stopped at an intersection. Due south, the road led to Maryland, only 5 miles distant. To the north only three miles, was the town of Oxford, a sleepy coach and train stop on the main line from Philadelphia to Baltimore. To the west, along a gravel road used mainly for moving farm animals and farm equipment, lay the tiny little village of Nottingham.

Edwin consulted his map: "This is it!" he exclaimed. Their buggy was resting in the middle of their new farmstead. It was prime dairy farm property, 160 acres of cleared meadows and crop fields, spotted with forested areas and sparkling creeks meandering across the farm on both sides of the main road to Oxford. Edwin's savings from years of toiling for the Scotts, along with Mary's generous dowry made it possible to acquire such choice land.

Mary and Edwin had been married early in the spring at Scott's Manor by a justice of the peace. Mary did not like the somber worship proceedings of the Friends, and Edwin felt that the Presbyterian rituals, while austere by Episcopalian standards, were too formal for him. They decided that the names and places of religious services were not important to them. Neither had been regular attendees in the places their parents had worshiped. They knew that when they had children, they must decide where their religious education would be provided, but this did not seem important now. Their priority was to take this property and make it a prosperous farm. The previous owner had built an attractive wooden farmhouse and sturdy barn with a tile silo.

After a few years, children arrived. Two boys and a girl were soon able to help with the small chores around the farm. Edwin and Mary also built two tenant houses and found families that were happy to have a roof over their heads in return for the heavy work of a hired hand. As the farm prospered, so did Edwin and Mary became prominent in the town of Oxford. Edwin became a director for the bank and the Grange. They joined the Oxford Friends Meeting. The children received their religious education with other local Quaker children in First Day's School, as it was so called by the Friends.

One day, Edwin visited the Chester County Courthouse in the pretty little town of West Chester. There had been some questions from a neighbor over the placement of the markers that delineated their boundaries. Edwin went to the office where deeds were recorded.

"Baily, you say?" asked the clerk. "That's not the usual spelling for a good English name."

Edwin had to agree, as well-intentioned people insisted on writing "Bailey" and had misspelled his name many times in his lifetime.

The clerk consulted a card catalog. "Wait a minute." said the clerk. "Here is the reference to your deed, and a half-dozen others using the name "Baily.""

Edwin peered at the cards, yellowed with age. "Some of these names look familiar." he said. "Jeremiah, Isaac, Joel…these are some of the names my grandmother had shown me on a page in our family bible." He remembered one name in particular, Joel, whom his grandmother said was the original Quaker immigrant from England. He asked to see the deed. There were several, as Joel Baily had annexed additional lands to the original farm. Then Edwin looked at the location. His property was less than 20 miles from his ancestor's first farm. "How ironic." he told the clerk. "Six generations of my family moving west to seek better land, and here I am where it all began."

He returned to his pickup truck, a 1914 Ford Model T Roadster with the turtleback removed and replaced with a wooden pickup box. He pointed the truck westward toward Oxford, but made a slight detour. Crossing the Brandywine River, which was but a creek as it wound its way past West Chester, he took a two-lane road named redundantly, "Street Road." Halfway down the road he approached the spot where the deed said Joel Baily had built his farm. He scanned the mailboxes for familiar surnames, cousins twice and thrice removed that Mama had shown him scrawled in the family Bible. There were none.

Where have they all gone? he thought. *To places even more remote than Missouri or Kansas? And why?* He received no answers to those thoughts, and continued his way back to his wife and children.

Edwin would move no more. He moved his spinster sister, Fannie back from Kansas to become the bookkeeper for his farm. Years later he had the bodies of his mother and father disinterred from the plot in Spring Hill, and reburied at Penn Hill Meetinghouse among others in the family. He finally felt at home.

Penn Hill Meetinghouse, Wakefield, Lancaster County

Chapter 16

COPING WITH THE TWENTIETH CENTURY

The stirrings of war in Europe were already affecting many in the United States by 1914. Even though America had not yet entered the war, factories in the big cities were humming with supply orders for the Allies fighting on French and German soil. Jobs were plentiful, and Edwin found it difficult to find strong men for fieldwork, even though he provided the families with very attractive tenant homes. The homes were small, but each family had plenty of land to raise their own vegetables and chickens. The families that occupied the two tenant houses now were headed by men in their Forties, robust in health, but not as energetic as the younger men. Fortunately, both families had many offspring. During harvest season, Edwin was able to utilize the girls and boys for a wide variety of chores.

Edwin's own children were growing strong as well. His oldest son, Joe, was now eight years old, and little brother Bill, six. Edwin and Mary's only daughter, Edith, was the baby, only three years old. Edwin felt fortunate, as his sons were safe from conscription in the Army. This was a growing possibility for other young men, as America was very likely to enter the war. Edwin himself had already served his county in the Spanish-American War in 1898, although it was over before he could confront the enemy. He was considered too old now to serve.

Besides, America needed the produce from her farms to feed her own growing population and those in Europe. Europe's farm fields were devastated by the armies moving from trench to trench in the agonizingly slow and bloody battles for territory.

Ever since the sinking of the *Lusitania,* there had been pressure from many Americans to join the war. Edwin recalled how the sinking of the *Maine* had stirred his patriotic fervor, even though his Quaker teachings said that he should turn the other cheek. Edwin still could not embrace that tenet in his relationship with God. The German-decent Amish and Mennonites in Pennsylvania were deeply pacifist and against the war. The fact that the country we would ultimately take up arms against was their former homeland no doubt colored their opinions.

In early 1917 President Wilson asked Congress to declare war on the Central Powers, as the alliance of Germany, Austria and the Ottoman Empire were called. It took another year and a half of bloody fighting for all sides to realize that fighting would not produce a decisive victory. An Armistice was declared in the fall of 1918.

The next decade saw great prosperity for the American people. Music and dress reflected the unbridled optimism of the people. Hemlines were raised, the music was upbeat, and all seemed right in the world.

Edwin's farm prospered. He invested in the very latest machinery to improve the output of his 160 acres. Tractors, harvesters, milking machines and other contraptions made it possible to run the farm with only one tenant farmer, and the sporadic help of his sons, when they were not in school. He renamed his farm *Modern Acres* to reflect the spirit of his investments.

In 1927 Edwin's eldest son, Joe, entered Pennsylvania State College to study agriculture. "State," as locals called it, had one of the finest agricultural schools in the nation. "State" was located in a beautiful spot, dead in the center of the state with views of the Appalachian ranges on all sides. It took five hours for Edwin and Mary to drive the Oldsmobile with their son up the winding roads to State College, Pennsylvania. When they departed for home, Joe smiled. At last on his own!

Joe was a good-looking young man, with sandy hair and gray-blue eyes. He had an eye for a pretty girl, too. He joined a fraternity and tried to balance the party weekends with his weekday studies. He was not a scholar, but easily passed all of his required courses and was on track to graduate on time in the four-year curriculum.

In his senior year several significant events occurred, one pleasant, one ominous. On a pleasant note, he became serious with an "import", a young woman from another college that he had met while at home in Oxford. She was from Wilmington, Delaware, about 35 miles distant from Oxford. She was a dark-haired beauty and loved a good party herself.

On an ominous note, even with the isolation of the Penn State campus, students became aware that the economy of the world was heading to rock bottom. "Black Tuesday," the meltdown of the stock market, had occurred in October of 1929, but many outside the financial world were not affected seriously until about 1931. Unemployment in parts of the country reached 25%. Joe realized that it was going to be difficult to find a job.

Joe really did not want to start farming, at least not right away. His major was in Agricultural Economics, and he wanted to enter a related field, such as feed and grain sales, or agricultural equipment. He did not plan to join his father in the day-to-day care of over a hundred head of cattle. His father had ample help from the tenant farmers.

Upon graduation, Joe enlisted as an Air Cadet in the US Army Air Corps. He was sent to a Texas flight school. Airplanes fascinated Joe. He loved to soar over the grasslands of East Texas in his PT-17 Trainer. He made it easily through basic training. In advanced flight school, competition was tougher. After 4 months he washed out and returned to Pennsylvania to seek other work. Later in life he would return to flying, as a private pilot.

Upon his return, he looked up his "import," the girl from Wilmington, Delaware. Meta Stewart was the daughter of a banker, a banker who had the good fortune to work for one of the few banks that did not close their doors during the Great Depression. Meta's and Joe's families were both fairly well insulated from the most devastating aspects of the Depression, although everyone lived frugally. Joe found a job selling life insurance in his hometown of Oxford. Joe and Meta were married that year.

Chapter 17

LIFE DURING THE DEPRESSION AND WORLD WAR

Joe and Meta moved into a furnished apartment in the center of the small town of Oxford. It was located in a large, attractive multistoried brick building along Broad Street. Broad Street was accurately named; a wide boulevard lined with oak trees, each home having an expansive lawn. Every lawn also sported a large vegetable garden, as everyone now needed to stretch his or her incomes. The larger homes had also converted parts of their buildings into apartments for the extra income.

To further supplement the family income, Meta sold children's clothing out of the apartment. This was accomplished much like the Tupperware and Avon sales concepts of a later day: Invite a few friends over for tea, with the clothing displayed conspicuously around the room. The clothing was machine-made, but of high quality and could be passed down from child-to child. It was a nice little side job, and Meta dressed her own children in the same outfits, enjoying the nice discount that came to the sales agents like herself.

By 1938, Meta and Joe had three children, two sons and a girl. The apartment would no longer do. With the help of the Meta's father, they secured a mortgage and built a large house on the edge of town. Joe gave up on the insurance business. The income was uncertain and he did not enjoy pressing other families with modest incomes to sign up for policies they could hardly afford. Joe went to work for his Dad on the farm, taking over the principal management and the bulk of the harder work. Edwin was now 58 years old, and while he still could handle a team of mules, he was grateful to leave the tossing of 80 pound bales of hay, and 100 pound sacks of grain to his older son. His younger son, Bill, would soon graduate from Cornell's large animal veterinary program. Bill would have plenty of clients in Chester County, which was principally agricultural.

Other than the extra belt-tightening, life went on fairly normally in farm communities during the Great Depression. Prices for their milk and other produce were not what the farmers hoped, but then again, the prices for their supplies were likewise low. While the Bailys were dairy farmers, they also raised a few hogs, chickens, and beef cattle to feed their own families. Entertainment was of the simplest forms: a Church social, family picnics, swims in the ponds or creeks. The big splurge was watching the Saturday matinee in one of the two local movie theaters, only 10 cents for kids. Evenings were spent listening to the radio mystery programs.

In the cities, life was not as idyllic. Soup lines were common, and were populated with out of work laborers and former white-collar workers. The closest city to Oxford was Wilmington, Delaware. Meta made frequent trips there with her brood. Her mother and father lived just outside the central area, near the city zoo. The children loved the trips. The sights and sounds of the city contrasted with the quiet countryside of Chester County, Pennsylvania.

In 1939, World War II was thrust upon America. Again, there was great reluctance to join the Allies. The scars of World War I were heavy on the minds of many Americans. Veteran's hospitals were still treating patients exposed to gas warfare, loss of limbs, and other horrible wounds of the lengthy conflict. Initially, the War lifted the country out of the Great Depression, as factories began to produce arms and ammunition for the Allies. Then, in December 1941, the Japanese attacked Pearl Harbor. America was committed to a war across two oceans.

Farmers such as Joe Baily were deferred from the draft. As in World War I, food for the troops and our ally nations became high priority. Again there was a shortage of manpower to work the fields, as thousands of young men put on uniforms. Later in the war, German prisoner labor was used to supplement the hands at harvest. It was a frightening sight to see soldiers with carbines standing watch over the laboring Germans in the gentle farmlands of Chester County.

The scariest things for the children were the air raid drills at night. Even though Oxford was hardly a strategic target for the Axis Powers, the War Department reasoned that an enemy pilot could use the pattern of lights to navigate to important manufacturing centers, or military bases. Every several weeks, the sirens would howl. Families hastened to draw the shades, and extinguish all but the faintest of lights. Joe was the Air Raid Warden for the street. He would put on his armband, and knock on the doors of houses that failed to comply. Though Germany had no warplanes that could reach across the Atlantic, the memory of Pearl Harbor was vivid on the minds of all Americans, and everyone was very diligent in observing the blackouts.

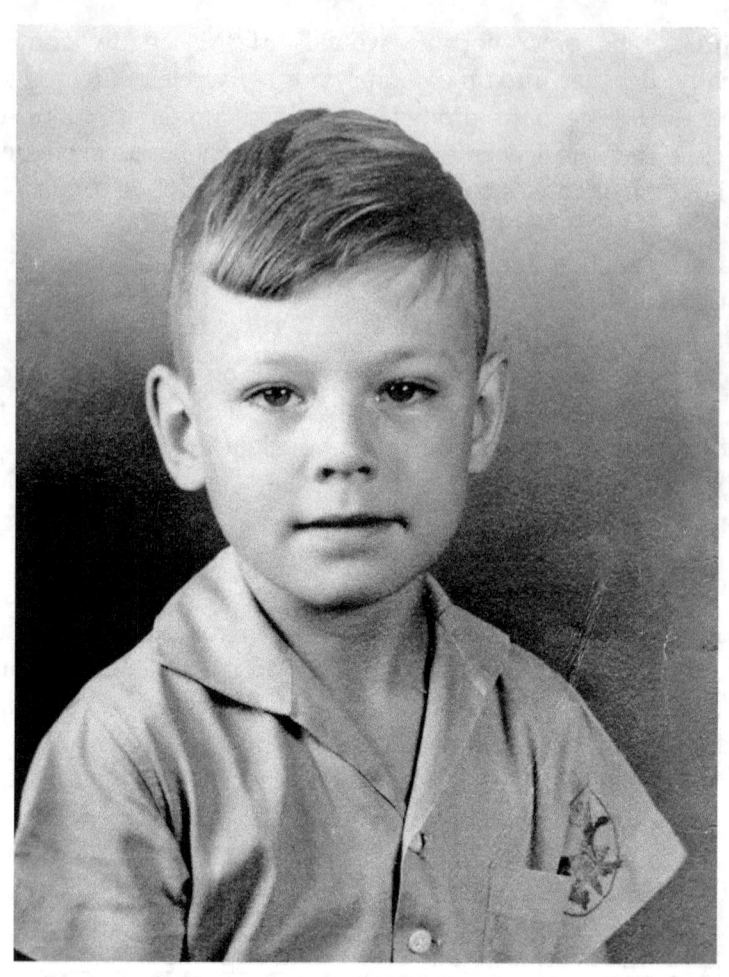

A Wartime Child
(The Author)
Combat insignia on the sleeve were iron-on, commonly packed
in cereal boxes during the war

Even the Quaker families sent their sons to war, although most chose non-combatant roles as quartermasters or corpsmen. Of course these jobs were often just as dangerous, if not more so, as carrying a carbine, but it satisfied the consciousness of the more traditional members of the Society of Friends. No one could deny that Germany and Japan must be stopped. The atrocities witnessed by our troops across the Atlantic and the Pacific were communicated in letters to their families. Everyone realized that this was not just wartime propaganda.

Finally, the war was over. America's sons and daughters returned. While there were not enough jobs for all, the GI Bill provided a wonderful alternative: Four years of higher education for all those who had served honorably. It was a very astute Act of Congress. By the time the first of the GI's finished college, America's economy was humming, and the country began a period of growth never equaled in her history.

Chapter Eighteen

LIFE IN A SMALL PROTESTANT TOWN

By the early Twentieth Century there were a variety of religious denominations in the town of Oxford, principally of English Protestant origin. The Friends, Amish, and Mennonites remained mostly in the countryside, tending their farms. The town merchants were primarily Baptists, Methodists, and Presbyterian. The Friends by then were the smallest congregation in town. Joe and Meta faced a dilemma of how to provide for the Christian education of their children. Joe and Meta went to Meetings infrequently, primarily for weddings and funerals. During the long periods of silence, their children would squirm and complain. There were a few attempts to place the children in First Day's School, but none of the other children in the class were familiar to the Baily children.

Joe and Meta were not concerned about attendance at services for appearances' sake. How one conducted one's life was the important thing. But they felt it was necessary to learn the stories of the Old and New Testament. Finally, the Presbyterian Church was chosen for Sunday School. It was the closest to home, and most of their Sunday School classmates were neighbors' children. The Presbyterian Church was very imposing: a large brick building with stained glass windows, and a tall steeple. It also had a huge pipe organ and choral group that boomed out hymns that could be heard from blocks away. This was quite a difference from the quiet, plain Meetinghouses that the children had known.

By the 1950's there were five children in Joe and Meta's family, one daughter and four sons. It was a time of prosperity again for most of the world. Even the conquered nations of the Axis Powers were rebuilding, with help from their former opponents. Music and dress again reflected the mood of the nation, this time with rock and roll and outlandish hairstyles.

Many a fiery preacher would set up tents and prayer meetings to capture the lost souls of Oxford, but when the singing was over, few made it to the front to be saved. The Quaker and English reserve permeated the town, even for the other Protestant groups. One male did not hug another, even his own dad. A smile and a handshake conveyed the same love, although it was always unspoken. Daughters got a peck on the cheek and a squeeze if they were lucky.

Most of the sons and daughters of Oxford eventually left the town after finishing their schooling. The more academically talented went to college or trade schools, and usually found jobs in other states where there was a heavier concentration of industry, such as New Jersey or Delaware. And of course, the Armed Forces reaped a good harvest from these strong young farm boys. The draft was on and the world was becoming tense. First Korea, then Vietnam and always the Cold War threat from the Soviet Union. Oxford's youth were exposed to the ugliness of modern war and to the fascinating capital cities of Europe and Asia. As Oxford's youth became worldlier, the exodus accelerated.

Fortunately, the farms did not need many people to keep in

operation. Mechanization of agriculture had reached the point where two adults could easily manage a farm of 200 acres, the average size in that area. Another census came and went and the population of the town was the same. The State of Pennsylvania built a bypass around the town to speed up the traffic from Baltimore to Philadelphia and Wilmington. Oxford's isolation was now nearly complete. Once a popular stop on the way between cities, it was now primarily a replenishment center for the farmers and mushroom growers. A potato chip factory just outside of town was Oxford's largest employer, and still is to this day. However, the residents of Oxford Township love the peaceful environment that they share.

Chester County, Pennsylvania is still a delightful place to live or just visit. Oxford and its surrounding towns are becoming increasingly suburbanized, with small developments springing up in former pastures or cornfields. Zoning laws have been passed, but developers are clever and find ways around the intent of the laws. The I-95 superhighway, just 10 miles south of the borough line, provides a quick commute into Baltimore, Maryland and Wilmington, Delaware. City families looking to raise their children in an area free from pollution and violent crime are see their solution in the countryside. They patiently car pool behind Amish horse and buggies on their way to the major highways. The pleasant smell of fresh-cut alfalfa mingles with the aroma of freshly spread cow manure, yet they do not seem to care.

Chapter Nineteen

ODYSSEY'S END AND NEW BEGINNING

The odyssey of this branch of a regularly practicing Quaker family ends here. Most of the younger generation in our family would not recognize the name George Fox, or even their common ancestor, Joel Baily. Yet, they somehow understand that the right thing to do is to follow their own hearts when it comes to the important decisions of right and wrong, and to the interactions with their fellow human beings. The heart is an incredibly accurate barometer of whether or not you are on the right path. The two weavers' sons, George and Joel, instilled this in those around them, and those that followed them. They called it the Inner Light. But the concept goes by other names in other faiths and is even known to the faithless. This was the grand legacy of the weavers of Wiltshire, who wove the fabric of cloth, and of human interaction. This branch of Joel's ancestors followed this Light across oceans, rivers, mountains, and prairies, and incredibly returned to within miles of the site of Joel's first homestead.

I was the middle child in the family of Joe and Meta Baily,

with all the benefits and drawbacks that accrue with being a middle child. My Great-Aunt Fannie, Edwin's sister, was the one who would frequently remind me of my heritage, and how it was important to understand the hardships of the generations that brought us our freedom and prosperity. I went to my share of Meetings as a child, and squirmed like my brothers and sister. The rough woolen suits that were then so popular with mothers made a young boy miserable on a hard wooden pew. Even so, I somehow realized that something profound was happening in that room. People said something only if they felt they had something important to share, not to fill the space of time. Even the periods of silence were welcome to these Friends, whose busy lives as farmers left little time to reflect on the greater meaning of their lives.

When I graduated from college, I entered the military to serve my country, as did all of my brothers. The fact that there was still a Draft during all those years certainly helped prompt my patriotism. When I arrived at Officer's Candidate School in Newport, Rhode Island, I stood in lines for my shoes, books, underwear, and all of the necessities for the making of a gentleman and an officer. In the last line, a petty officer was operating a metal stamping machine. I recognized that the small ovals he was stamping were "dog tags." He asked me for my name and blood type, and began working on the shiny metal objects. Then he looked up and asked "Religion?" I was taken aback. I had been ambiguous about religious affiliation for most of my life since I was a teenager. Now I was going to have it stamped in steel! I thought for a moment back to the times when I had meaningfully reflected on why I was placed in this world. After a pause, I replied confidently: "Society of Friends."

Soon after, I was commissioned, and began my own odyssey with a new wife, and a whole world in which to wander. There are few places on this earth that we have not explored.

The Light still beckons.

The Weavers' Legacy

EPILOGUE

When my father and mother retired, the land was sold to an Amish family, who lovingly cares for the soil still using horse-drawn equipment. The Baily grandchildren and great-grandchildren that followed found employment that did not require a farmer's every-day, early-morning rising. However they loved to visit the farm on holidays, and did so until it was finally sold.

I asked my father prior to the sale, why did he not sell earlier and enjoy the sizable sum the farm was worth, earlier in life. He replied: "Because I enjoy farming!" I am happy that he finally found contentment in the work, not of his first choosing.

Toward the end of his life, my father attended Meetings on a more regular basis, at the encouragement of his granddaughter. We joked that he was cramming for the finals. Meta and Joe were buried in the family plot at Penn Hill Meetinghouse among other generations of their family. It is a very peaceful setting.

Many of the early tenets of the Society of Friends, such as serving in combat, were changing. Edwin never got a chance to fire a shot in anger, but there were many Quakers who did so, in earlier and later wars.

What of William Penn's encouragement of Quakers, and other faiths to settle in Pennsylvania? The Society of Friends has only about 300,000 professed adherents in the world, but there are still a surprising number of Friends Meetings in Pennsylvania and many other states and countries. The Quakers are more assertive than they were in the early days of the movement, and despite their small numbers make a big impact on the world stage. The American Friends Service Committee is an organization that promotes social justice and humanitarian causes all over the world. Today's Friends are less likely to be farmers, and more likely to be city-living social activists. The somber garb that their ancestors wore, and the quiet familiar method of addressing one another is gone. Today's Friend may wear a Greenpeace T-shirt, shouting slogans. Two of our recent American Presidents have sent their young children to Friends schools while in office.

William Penn's more important legacy is the tolerance for other faiths and cultures that he insisted upon in his new province. The German immigrants that quickly followed the Quakers still practice today their farming and their faith in the old way, and live in harmony with their neighbors with cars, electronic gadgets, and modern appliances. Later waves of immigrants arrived from Europe and became the workforce for the extensive mining and manufacturing operations that pervade the mountain towns and the big cities in Pennsylvania. Ethnic groups of all cultures thrive.

It is difficult to conceive the amazing acts of bravery, love, faith, and luck that must occur for the human race to move forward and extend their footprint on this earth. The characters in this book represent just one branch of by now many hundreds, perhaps thousands, of descendents of Joel Baily. Each has a story, and their survival is a triumph.

AUTHOR'S NOTES

The characters in this book are real. The members of the Baily family have been researched thoroughly, and while I did find some inconsistencies, the path of migration is documented fairly well in an exhaustive genealogy done in the early 1900's. It is entitled *Genealogy of the Baily Family,* compiled by Gilbert Cope, and since expanded on multiple sites on the Internet. A cousin supplied me with a book published by her cousin William J. Scarlett entitled *The Baily–Scarlett Connection, A History Compilation from 1684.* The historical figures such as George Fox and William Penn are, likewise, well documented in multiple sources. With regard to the practices of the Quakers after the emigration, I relied on a scholarly work by Thomas D. Hamm entitled *The Quakers in America*, Columbia University Press, 2003.

The dialogues, motivations, and musings of the characters are the invention of the author. However, I believe that they are consistent with the customs of those days. I was fortunate to obtain letters and newspaper clippings from some of the characters dating to the mid-1800's, and I utilized portions of these in the text.

San Diego, California
December 30, 2011

www.ingramcontent.com/pod-product-compliance
Lightning Source LLC
Chambersburg PA
CBHW060208290526
45789CB00003B/1213